Ars longa,
vīta brevis est.

©2025 Emily Silversmith · North Landing Books · All Rights Reserved

The lovely illustrations in this collection come from Victorian-era books and academic journals on zoology and botany. I have selected images that offer that vintage look, yet are detailed, clear, sharp, and realistic. Birds in this collection are mostly colorful, but not too exotic - since we need simple and smooth outlines easy to cut out.

The pictures you will find on these pages fall into two groups:

• Bird images, easy to cut out for decoupage and collaging. I digitally isolated each one from its original background, placed it on white, and lightly color-corrected it to restore the original look.

• Half- or full-page images of plants or birds on branches. In terms of their outlines, these are more complex no-background images that can be either cut out (whole or in pieces - a bit more work than the solo bird images!), or used as a background for your collage work. I also frame them for interior decoration. For these illustrations I retained the vintage paper color in the background.

Besides decoupage, you can use these illustrations for school projects, scrapbooking, junk journaling, and greeting card making. You can also collage them for many genres of mixed media art.

Happy crafting, beautiful one!

Emily Silversmith

Booah Nawa Nawa
Borrong Brass Brass

Perlasan – Boorong Radja Oodang
(Kingsfisher)

Aleurites moluccana
Booah Cras – Boorong Booak Busik

پوکوء بواه لڠست ― بورڠ چرچڤ

Poko Booah Langsat ― Boorong Chichap

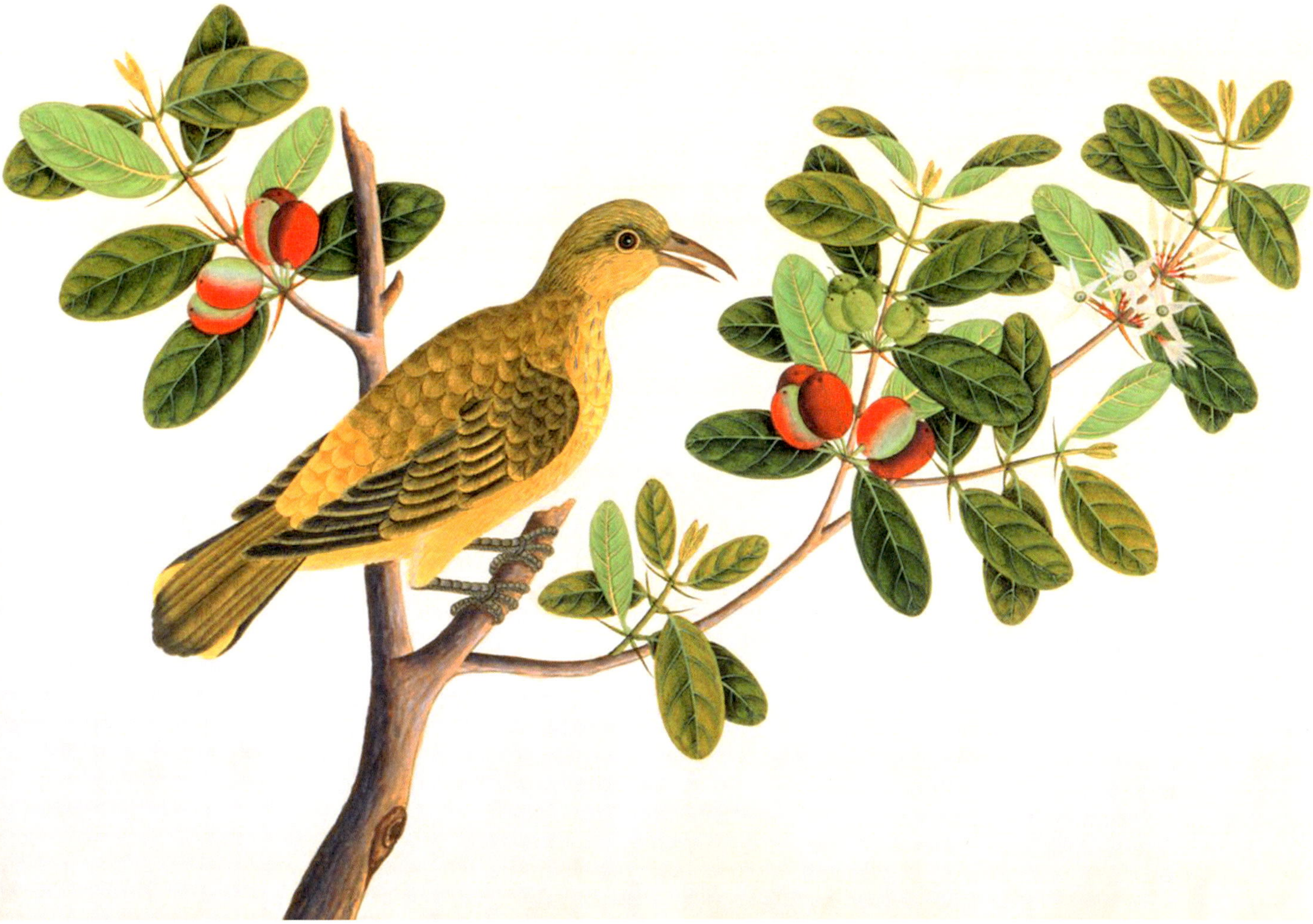

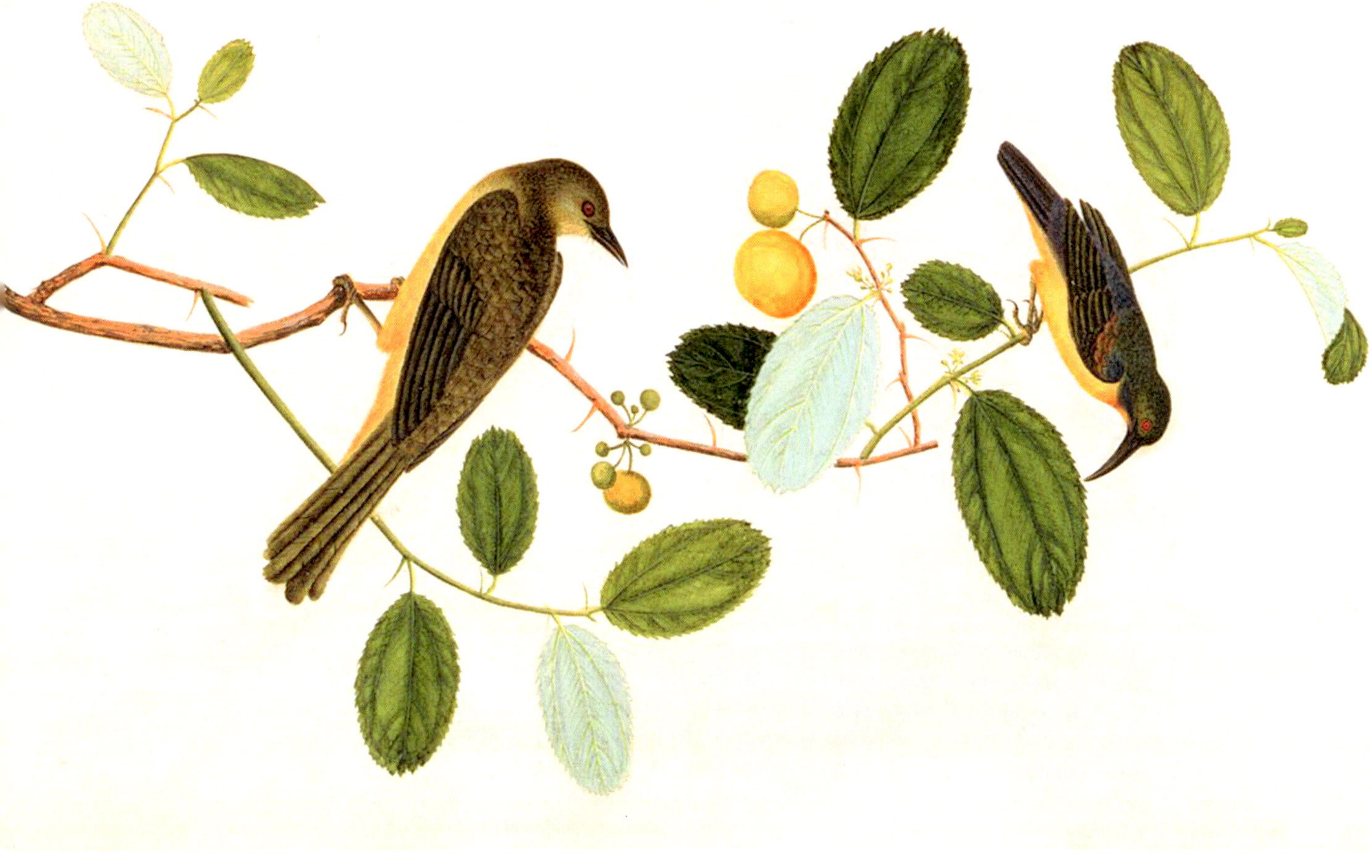

Boorong koonjit koonjit
Jamboo Flore Mera — Eugenia Malaccensis

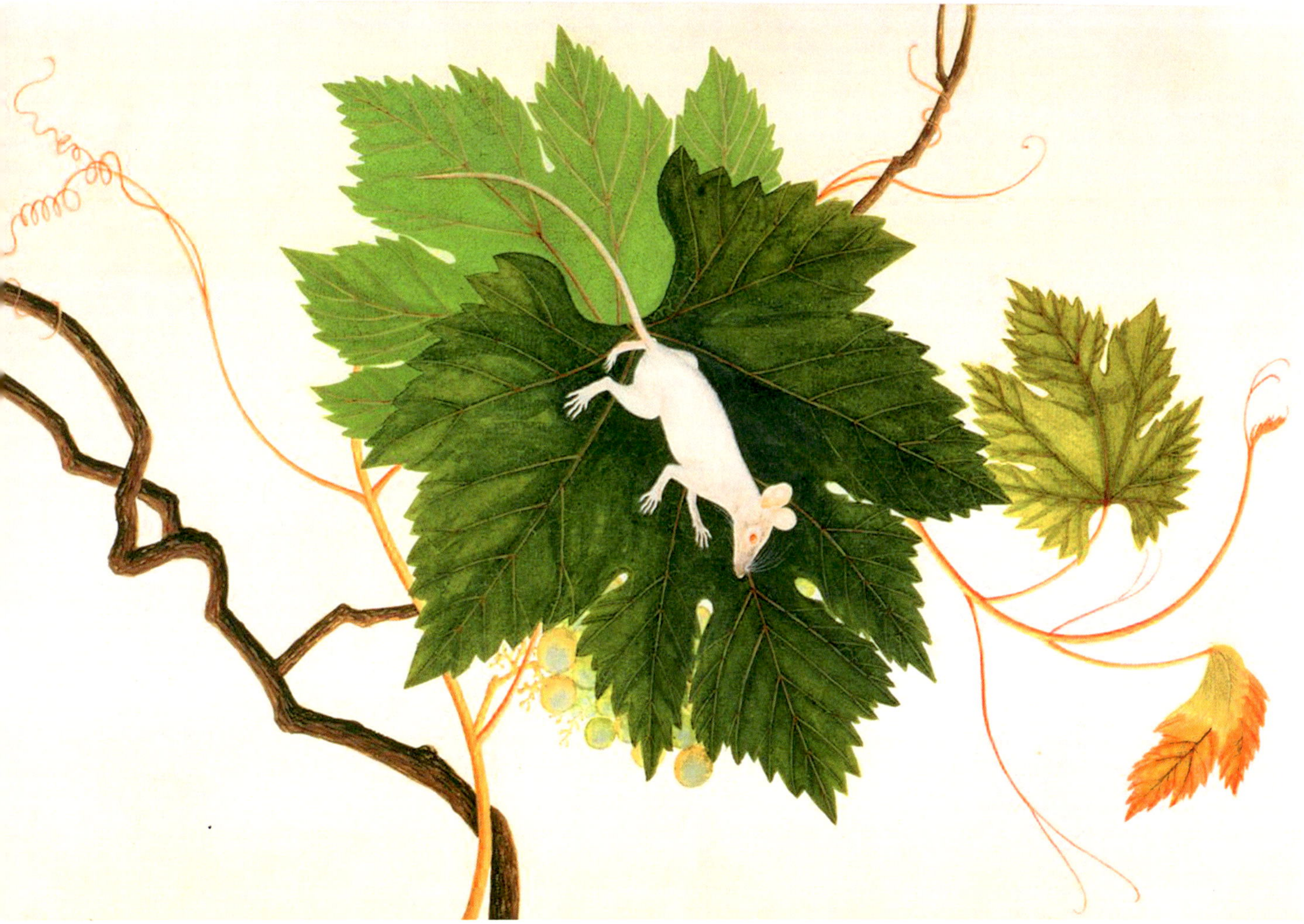

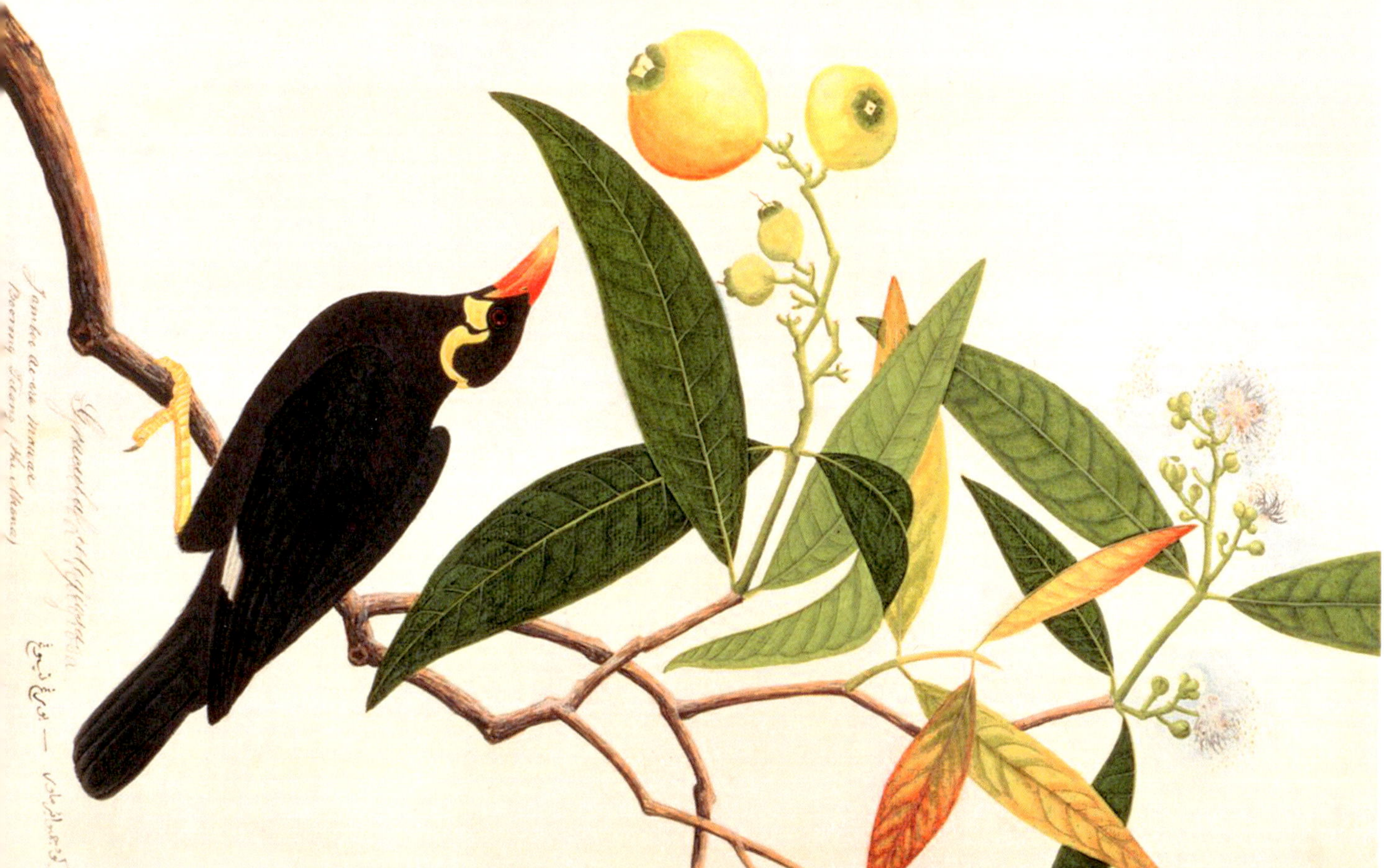

Bastard Pulasang

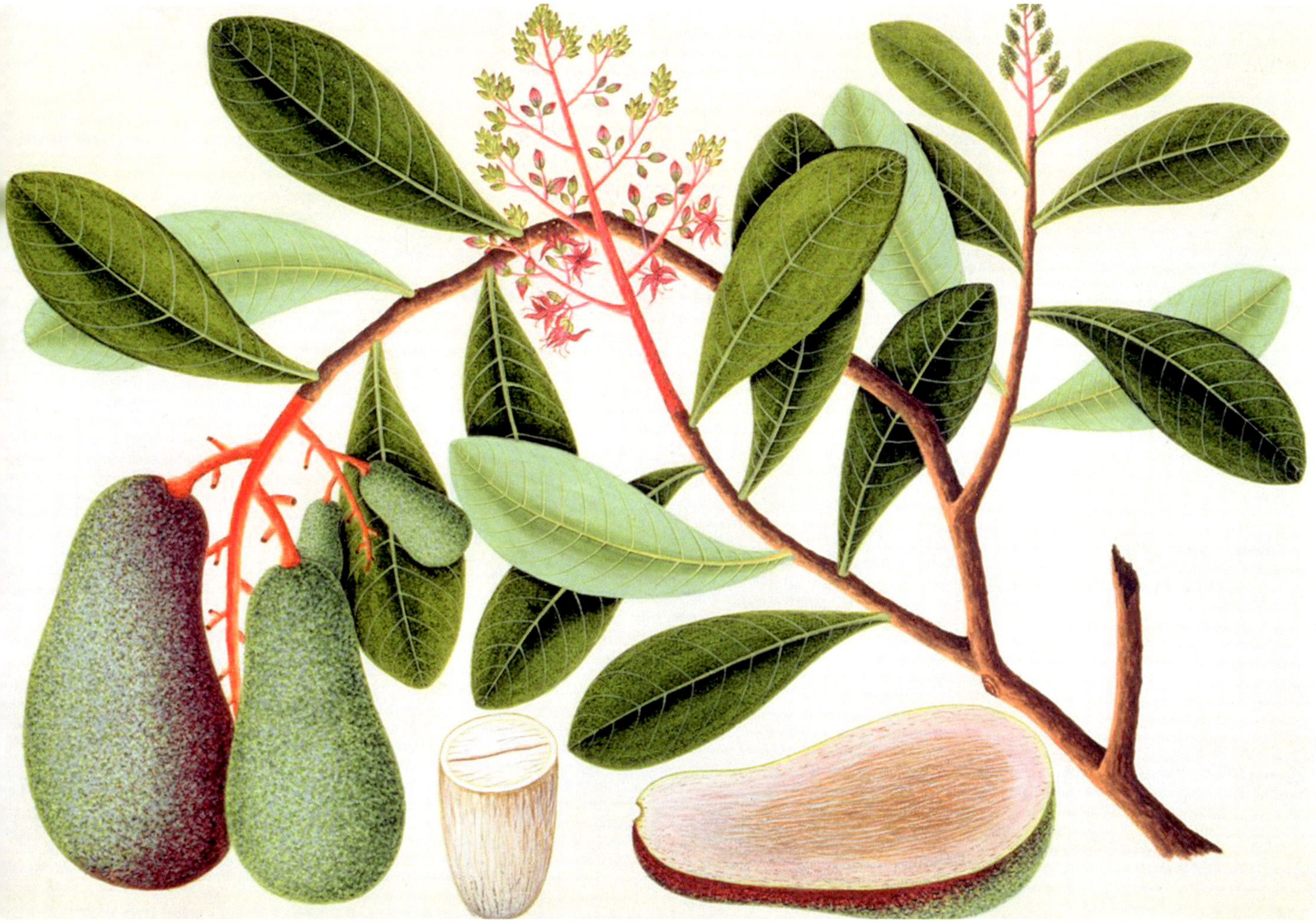

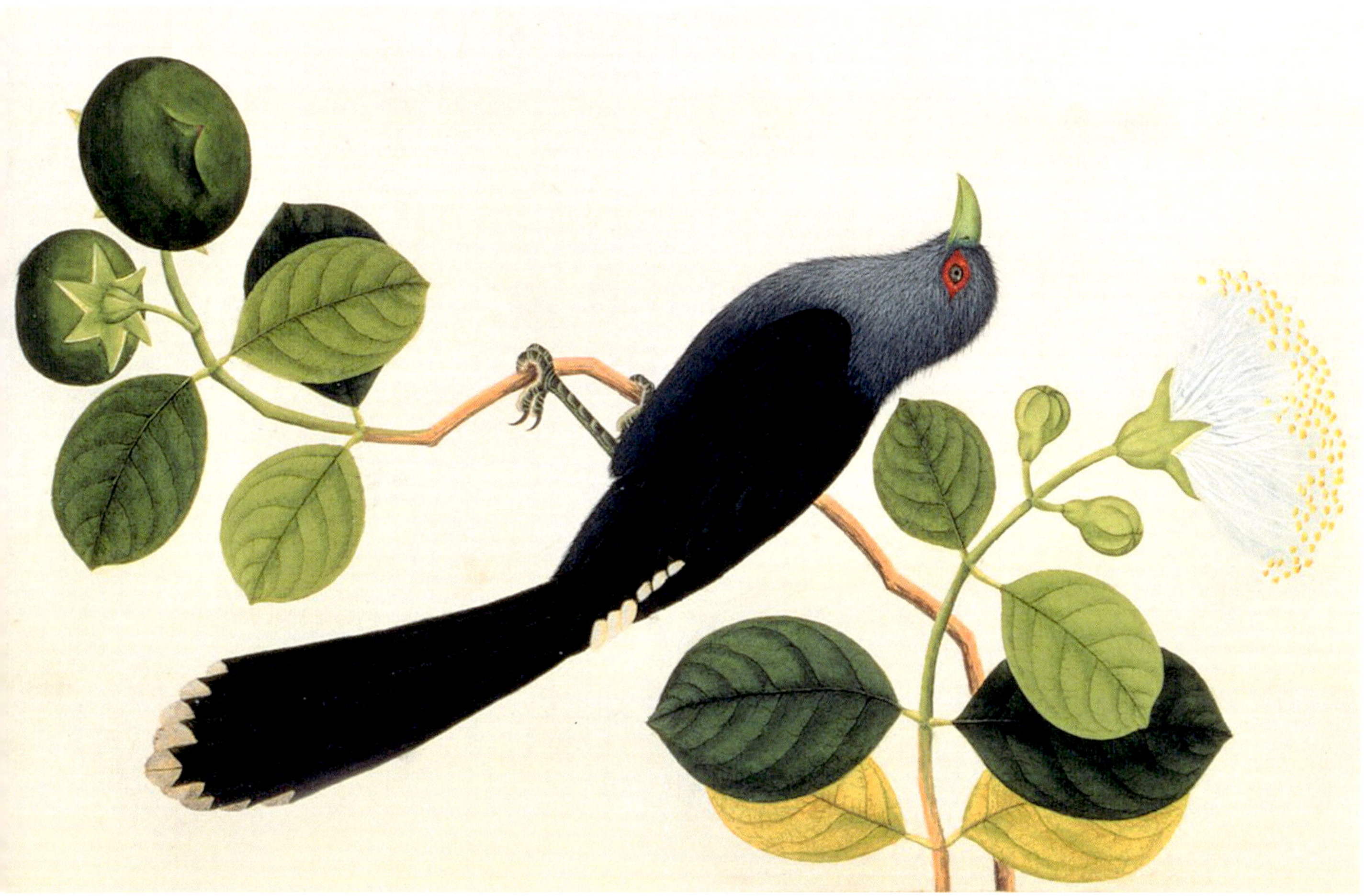

www.ingramcontent.com/pod-product-compliance
Lightning Source LLC
LaVergne TN
LVRC091354060526
838201LV00042B/415